Leadership and Adoption of Instructional Technology in Schools

Curtis D. Brandon Sr.

DISSERTATION.COM

Boca Raton

Leadership and Adoption of Instructional Technology in Schools

Copyright © 2008 Curtis D. Brandon Sr.
All rights reserved. No part of this book may be reproduced or transmitted in any form or by any means, electronic or mechanical, including photocopying, recording, or by any information storage and retrieval system, without written permission from the publisher.

Dissertation.com
Boca Raton, Florida
USA • 2008

ISBN-10: 1-59942-674-9
ISBN-13: 978-1-59942-674-7

Leadership and the Adoption of
Instructional Technology in Schools

by
Curtis D. Brandon

An Applied Dissertation Submitted to the
Fischler School of Education and Human Services
in Partial Fulfillment of the Requirements
for the Degree of Doctor of Education

Nova Southeastern University
2008

Abstract

Leadership and the Adoption of Instructional Technology in Schools. Brandon, Curtis D., 2008: Applied Dissertation, Nova Southeastern University, Fischler School of Education and Human Services. Instructional Technology (1966 1978)/Leadership/Organizations (Groups)/Distance Education

This applied dissertation was designed to investigate the characteristics most represented in two school districts, an inner-city and a suburban district. These characteristics were related to the innovativeness of the school district and the perception of individual leadership in schools that have passed the performance criteria for state accreditation. Forty schools and 200 principals were randomly selected to participate in the study for a period of 3 to 4 months.

The researcher used three instruments to determine whether differences existed between the two districts in regard to performance on the Standards of Learning assessments. He developed a checklist for interview questions on instructional technology strategies that might be implemented by leaders and teachers in the classroom. A Perceived Organizational Innovativeness Scale was used to measure the innovativeness of the school district, and an Individual Innovativeness Scale was used to measure the perception of individual leaders concerning the innovativeness of the school district.

The findings indicated that organization innovativeness contributed to the innovativeness of individuals, such as leaders. Leaders categorized by innovativeness contributed to the overall structure of the organization by means of social networks with predictable human behavior in the organization. The passing of the Standards of Learning assessment and the schools' proven performance and accreditation status were clearly related to the behavioral patterns of individual and the social networks implemented by the leadership.

Table of Contents

	Page
Chapter 1: Introduction	1
Theoretical Background	2
Rationale for the Study	2
Focus of Instructional Technology Adoption	5
Inner-City District	5
Suburban District	7
Limitations	8
Chapter 2: Review of Related Literature	9
The Problem	9
Definition of Leadership	10
Documentation of the Problem	13
School Teams Achieving Results for Students	14
Significance of the Study	18
Relationship of the Problem to the Literature	19
Accreditation Process	20
Accountability and Leadership	22
Diffusion Theory and Instructional Technology	23
Innovation Decision Process	24
Individuals' Innovativeness and School Districts' Innovativeness	25
Innovativeness Adoption Categories	26
Applying Rogers' Five Categories to School Faculty	27
Leadership	29
Reasons Teachers Use Computer Technology	31
Raising Teachers' Motivation When Integrating Instructional Technology	32
Summary	33
Chapter 3: Methodology	35
Overview	35
Participants	35
Purpose of Project	36
Research Questions	37
Instruments	37
Procedure	38
Data Analysis	39
Summary	39
Chapter 4: Results	41
Demographic Profiles	41
Descriptive Statistics	45
Interview Findings	47
Findings Across All Interviewed Participants	48
Summary	51
Chapter 5: Discussion	53
Overview	53

Implications of the Findings 54
Quantitative Findings...54
Interview Findings 56
Summary of Findings...58
Limitations 58
Recommendations for Future Research 59
Summary 60

References 61

Appendixes
- A Calculation of Accreditation Ratings in Standards of Accreditation............66
- B Accrediting Public Schools (Verified Credits) 68
- C Bell-Shaped Curve 70
- D Perceived Organizational Innovativeness Scale 72
- E Individual Innovativeness Scale 76
- F Interview Technology Checklist 80
- G Interview Log of Contact Information 83

Tables
1. Performance Accreditation of Schools in the Suburban District, by Number...42
2. Performance Accreditation of Schools in the Inner-City District, by Number..42
3. Participants' Perceptions of Individual and Organization Innovativeness in the Inner-City District, by Number 43
4. Participants' Perceptions of Individual and Organization Innovativeness in the Suburban District, by Number 44
5. Descriptive Statistics for Measures of Innovativeness 45
6. Pearson's Correlation Statistics of Measures From the Perceived Organizational Innovativeness and Individual Innovativeness Scales for Two Districts..46
7. Participants' Responses to the Interview Technology Checklist, by Number ...49

v

Chapter 1: Introduction

The No Child Left Behind Act (NCLB) of 2001 has highlighted the importance of leadership for school success, mandated raising student performance levels, and demanded accountability of leaders (Wilson, 2001). The act covers all educational districts and requires public schools to raise student performance across the curriculum. The act also requires computer technology standards for all curricula and holds educational leaders responsible for communicating these standards to classroom teachers (Dillon, 2006; Miech, 2000).

This study focused on two school systems titled the inner-city district and suburban district. Both are in the southeastern United States. The three areas covered by this study involved the diffusion of innovation and the adoption process of instructional technology: (a) The researcher reviewed and classified the processes associated with individual and organizational innovation, (b) compared the characteristics associated with organizational leaders in schools where state accreditation had been attained and where principals and other leaders have supported the use of instructional technology (Simonson & Wheeler, 2003), and (c) assessed the similarities and differences between the organization and the leadership innovativeness approach in schools that failed to meet state standards. The researcher related these three areas to the performance of each school and indicated whether they successfully gained or failed to gain state accreditation. The study included 40 schools and 200 principals.

At the outset of this study, the researcher examined the literature that focuses on organizational leadership to discover whether the innovativeness of the organization corresponded to the use of instructional technology by teachers. A great deal of research was available on the diffusion of instructional technology (Couros, 2003). Researchers, however, have paid scant attention to how the relationships and dependencies among educational leaders and their organizations affect the adoption of instructional technology. For this study, the researcher addressed many critical factors that have influenced the dissemination of technology by using the diffusion theory and adoption theory.

Theoretical Background

Diffusion theory. According to Rogers (2003), "Diffusion is a process in which an innovation is communicated through channels over time among members of a social system" (p. 409). The diffusion process is a systematic approach to an organization's adoption of new technology. Many organizations have been compelled by the NCLB to participate in the diffusion process and acquire new technology.

Adoption theory. The adoption theory was instrumental in acquiring data about the innovations implemented by both individual school leaders and the organizations they represented. LaRose and Hoag (1996) noted that the adoption theory noted that, when plotted, the rate of adoption forms an S-shaped curve. This curve has a steep slope on the right and reflects individuals and organizations most receptive to new ideas.

Rationale for the Study

American school systems have invested dearly in the adoption of instructional technology for school buildings and classrooms. The technology inventory has accumulated considerably huge amounts of record keeping. Shuldman (2004) reported that the National Center for Educational Statistics conducted the Fast Response Survey in 1999 and found that 51% of teachers surveyed reported that they were moderately well prepared to use technology in the classroom, whereas 33% indicated that they were either well prepared (23%) or very well prepared (10%).

In a study of New Hampshire teachers, Shuldman (2004) used the Levels of

Technology Implementation scale, developed by Moersch in 1995, to measure a teacher's level of technology use on a 6-point rating scale where 0 = *nonuse* and 6 = *refinement*. Shuldman found that 31% of the New Hampshire teachers responded that their integration of technology was at Level 3 or higher; nationally, 28% of teachers responded at the same level. In the New Hampshire study, 69% of the teachers indicated levels of 0 to 2; 32% scored at Level 2, indicating the need to be cautious when adopting; and 21% scored at the Level 0, indicating a failure to use instructional technology integration.

According to Rogers' (2003) theory of innovation decisions, the process of socially adopting or rejecting an innovation by individuals or organizations in a social system may be based on the individual or the entire social system. One factor that is essential is administrative support and leadership.

This study focused on opinion leadership. Rogers (2003) defined this term as the degree an individual is able to influence the attitudes and behaviors of other individuals with relative frequency. He characterized opinion leadership as an informal position associated with social status and believed, "[It] is earned and maintained by the individual's technical competence, social accessibility, and conformity to system's norms" (p. 27). The most outstanding characteristic of opinion leadership is the ability to communicate or network among peers within the social environment of the organization. Rogers also found that both opinion leadership and leaders who oppose changes may be found in many organizations.

The study of Rogers (2003) raised two questions. They are as follows: (a) Is there a relationship between the leadership styles of school districts passing state standards accreditation, and (b) is the leadership in a school district that is passing state accreditation characterized by the opinion leadership styles and characterized as technical competencies, social accessibility, and conformity to the norms of school district?

According to Vitale (2005), the process of development and organization may become the basic framework for mastering what is not known about instructional technology for leaders when an organization is integrating instructional technology. In a study of the spread of an educational innovation among 38 school superintendents in Pittsburgh, an overhaul of the math curriculum for the public schools brought about innovations that included textbooks, audiovisual aides for teaching new concepts, and summer institutions to train teachers in new subject areas.

The new math innovation spread relatively quickly and was reinforced by the National Science Foundation in conjunction with the U.S. Department of Education (Rogers, 2003). Educators accepted modern math as an improvement to the curriculum. Of the 38 school superintendents, only one adopted the innovations in 1958 without any interpersonal network links from fellow colleagues. Six friends constituted a group that developed the framework while interacting inside and outside of normal obligations. The efforts of these six friends played a significant role in the diffusion of modern math in the Pittsburgh public schools.

Once the group members (opinion leaders) adopted the math innovations, the rate of adoption increased tremendously (Rogers, 2003). According to Rogers, only one adoption took place in 1958 (innovator). This single adoption increased to 5 in 1959, 15 in 1960, 27 in 1961, 35 in 1962, and 38 in 1963. Characteristics associated with opinion leadership styles include conformity to the norms of the social system, serving as role models, and accessibility. Rogers asserted that understanding the processes of diffusion and opinion leadership characteristics may form a basic framework and may serve as a guide for school districts.

Focus of Instructional Technology Adoption

Surry (1997) indicated that the focus of adoption of instructional technology is human perceptions. This was the reason for adopting instructional technology for this study. A more gradual slope downhill on the left side of the S-shaped curve indicates schools with slower rates of adoption. In the years from 1984 to 1988, technology in some school districts was limited to two IBM clone computers.

However, both districts in this study have adopted many technological innovations in the last decade. The results of a survey conducted by the National Center for Education Statistics (2000) indicated the degree that teachers and administrators were using computers and were using instructional technology to access the Internet. All told, 34% of the respondents reported using technology to assist with administrative duties, and only 10% reported using instructional technology for classroom lessons, research, or best practices. Dikkers, Hughes, and McLeod (2005) wrote that technology has emerged so rapidly that a bridge has developed between educators and school leaders. Few mechanisms exist to prepare leaders for the ever-changing espousal of innovation in kindergarten through Grade 12 education.

Teachers have access to LCD projectors, scanners, digital cameras, videocassette recorders, and compact disc players. Clearly, adoption of instructional technology is not the obstacle preventing teachers from using computer technology. This applied dissertation study has attempted to discover (a) how innovative the organization is and how it perceives change, (b) whether individual leaders regard change favorably or unfavorably, and (c) what issues are facing the organization.

Inner-City District

Description of community. The inner-city district is located in the southeastern

United States. Through the area flow rivers that serve as the building blocks of the economy. The physical geography is marked by a fall line. The falls of the rivers have produced a site that has allowed for easy settlement and has become a foundation for economic development. Driven by law and finance, the inner-city district is home to an administrative center that includes both a U.S. Court of Appeals and a Federal Reserve district.

Inner-city district's population. According to the 2000 census, the population of the community was 996,512. Of residents who were 25 years old and older, 82.6% were high school graduates; 29.2% were college graduates. Median household income was $46,800, 6% above the U.S. average. The unemployment rate was 4.1%. The labor force numbered 540,102, and businesses have had low levels of unionization and union election activity.

Description of work setting. The community has adopted educational reforms titled Standards of Learning (SOL). This program sets high, clear, measurable academic standards on a statewide basis and then measures students' progress in meeting those standards. Students are tested in English, math, science, and history in the third, fifth, eighth grades and in high school. The work setting in this study is two middle schools. Each middle school has a principal, two assistant principals, two media specialists, and support staff. The ethnicity breakdowns of the two middle schools in the 2004-2005 school year was 88.95% Black, 7.36% White, 2.93% Hispanic, and less than 1% Asian and American Indian students. The operating budget for the inner-city district amounted to $287,028,365.

Demographics of the inner-city district. This public school district enrolls 25,222 students in 32 elementary schools, 10 middle schools, 9 high schools, 6 exceptional education schools, and 5 vocational and alternative schools. The high schools offer thematic programs in the arts, world languages, business, life sciences, math, science, and technology. Two of the schools in the community allow gifted students to take classes at area colleges and at a military school that is the nation's first public military school.

The Mathematics and Science Center promotes excellence in learning and teaching in math, science, and technology. The Governor's School for Government and International Studies has been a semifinalist in the National Academic Championship Quiz Bowl for the past 2 years. The city's Technical Center is an award-winning vocational technical school. Forty-five percent of contracted teachers have advanced degrees.

The schools feature distance learning classrooms and provide access to the Internet. Of the graduates, 53.6% received an advanced studies diploma and 72.9% plan to pursue postsecondary education. The district has 46 accredited private and parochial elementary and secondary schools that enroll nearly 14,000 students.

Suburban District

Description of community. The suburban district is a thriving community in the southeastern United States. In 2005, the community had an estimated population of 281,000 residents and was home to 22,000 businesses. The suburban district is growing. Its community recently earned an AAA bond rating from three agencies and is home to a newly built semiconductor plant and to one of the largest shopping centers in the United States. The suburban district's community has low taxes, good business opportunities, and excellent infrastructure. The newest additions include a home to Fortune 500 companies, technological innovations, and global business communication.

Statistics on the suburban district. The district enrolls 47,000 students in 43 elementary schools, 12 middle schools, 9 high schools, 2 technical centers, and an alternative school that houses elementary and middle school students. Demographically, the district has 51% White, 35.8% Black, 4.9% Asian, 3.6% Hispanic, and 4.7% other students. The operating budget is $411 million; the expenditure per pupil is $7,768.

Limitations

This study was not limited to principals from schools that contained all grade levels except kindergarten. Additionally, time was a factor in receiving information from designated school personnel through the mail.

Chapter 2: Review of Related Literature

The Problem

Statement of the problem. Some researchers perceived a lack of successful individual leadership and organizational innovativeness (De Leon, 2006; Mazzeo, 2003; Sanders, 2006). They contended that this lack of leadership and innovativeness has prevented the successful implementation of instructional technology to boost students' academic performance.

Description of the problem. Even though some literature supported this perceived lack of successful leadership and an effective use of innovativeness in organizations, results have indicated that, of 1,822 schools in the state, only 1,336 schools (73%) have met the goals of each district statewide, as expressed in the adequate yearly progress (AYP) report that measures the accreditation of school divisions based on students' overall SOL assessments for accreditation (Virginia Department of Education, 2006b). According to the Virginia Department of Education, the annual report card provides data on schools and school divisions that have or have not met the objectives required by the federal education law to reach 100% proficiency of all students in reading and mathematics by 2014. The report used in this study included data reflecting that 400 schools (22%) did not meet AYP standards and the status of 86 schools (5%) was yet to be determined.

In a breakdown of data for the two districts involved in this study, a report of the AYP for the inner-city district noted that the district did not meet the state's AYP standards. The report further addressed the local school division, the suburban district, where AYP standards were met. These findings caused the researcher to explore what might be generalized from these data and what factors or solutions might cause a differentiation in the two districts' data reports developed by the state department of education.

Definition of Leadership

For the purpose of this study, the term *leadership* has been defined as individuals (principals) in a school district who influence the attitude and behavior of individuals (teachers) informally with relative frequency. In this context, leadership is an informal status that usually is earned through technical competence, social accessibility, and the leader's conformity to the school district's norms (Rogers, 2003). In this study, the researcher found that this kind of individual leadership was recognized throughout the related literature and represented the opinion leadership aimed at school districts' principals.

According to Rogers (2003), "When the social system is oriented to change, the opinion leaders are more innovative but when the systems norm are opposed to change, the behavior of leaders also reflect the norm" (p. 27). This finding led the researcher to explore solutions to the following questions: (a) What may be assumed about leadership in school districts that are not passing state accreditation and the leadership characteristics, (b) what may be assumed about school districts passing state accreditation and leadership characteristics, and (c) are the communication networks effective in districts passing state accreditation? Rogers made a striking point that the position that opinion leaders have in their communication system or network links in a school system is unique and influential.

According to Clarke (1991) and to Ruebling, Stow, Kayona, and Clarke (2004), if school districts are not meeting performance standards for state accreditation, the behavior of the leadership is in question. In a study to determine the quality of a newly implemented curriculum for language arts and math, Ruebling et al. found that 143 classroom observations indicated that few teachers used the new curriculum, and only one third had acceptable lesson plans. In another category relating to leadership behavior deficiencies, these researchers indicated the following findings:

1. Only 25% focused on skills and concepts appropriate to new curriculum's sequence and score.

2. Fewer than 40% aligned teaching with the appropriate concepts or skills.

3. Fewer than 40% provided the right setting for students to use concepts or skills.

4. Only 33% of the teachers aligned the level of thinking to Bloom's taxonomy.

5. Fewer than half were knowledgeable of the subject.

Ruebling et al. (2004) found data from interviews with leaders in the systems that indicated these deficiencies:

1. No formal training was received by teachers on the new curriculum.

2. No formal system was established to process or monitor the new curriculum.

3. No system existed for evaluation or curriculum revisions.

4. Teachers were unable to discuss the results of assessments.

5. Teachers were unable to discuss the results of assessments.

6. Teachers were unable to discuss the difference in classroom instruction.

7. Teachers' expectations for using, communicating, and understanding the results were unmet.

According to these findings, the behavior of the leadership in the school system needed to change to improve the learning performance of a district.

In North Dakota, Feldner and Kincaid (2002) conducted a 5-year study on the process and movement of educators toward the integration of technology. Their methodology consisted of two professional development phases. One phase was to give teachers an opportunity to design current lessons or units that implemented the integration of technology, and the other was to increase leadership knowledge, the integration of technology, and modeling for the effective use of technology. The study used the Professional Competency Continuum (PCC) profile assessment; an assessment tool that is used to collect data on the behavior of educators based on national technology standards.

Upon completion of the PCC assessment, the North Dakota educators were placed on a continuum that consisted of three ranges: entry level, adoption level, and level of transformation. The range for educators signified the degree of experience that the educators had with the integration of technology standards at the national level. Feldner and Kincaid (2002) indicated that 9,120 educators in kindergarten through Grade 12 participated, or 89% of all of the full- and part-time educators.

The results for administrators indicated that their proficiency levels rated higher in PCC competency areas. The mean for the core competency areas for administrators was 4.71. Feldner and Kincaid (2002) found the following mean scores for each PCC competency area for administrators: (a) 3.98 for core technology skills; (b) 3.82 for curriculum, learning, and assessment; (c) 3.98 for classroom and instructional management; 3.95 for professional practice; and 5.04 for administrative competencies.

Support from opinion leaders in the field of education exemplifies characteristics associated with technology competence, accessibility, conformity, and the ability to be role models who inspire followers. Key characteristics are experienced by leaders in school districts that take advantage of their ability to plan for staff development. Facilitators of teacher training effectively teach instructors how to integrate technology into the curricula that encourage academic performance. Developing opinion leaders through communication channels linked by interconnecting individuals establishes a pattern that provides performance results acceptable to the performance and norms of a school district struggling to meet state accreditation standards (Rogers, 2003).

Documentation of the Problem

In considering how to document the problem, the researcher explored studies in related literature concerning the efforts made toward district staff development by school divisions for leadership training for school leaders when planning for the integration of instructional technology in the day-to-day work setting of school divisions. According to Dikkers et al. (2005), a 2000 statistical report of the National Center for Education Statistics indicated that few mechanisms exist in kindergarten through Grade 12 education to prepare school leaders to understand and espouse innovative technologies, even though technological innovation is occurring rapidly. Although nearly all public school teachers have access to computers or the Internet somewhere in their schools, only a third of them are well prepared or very well prepared to integrate the use of computers and the Internet in their teaching.

Concerning district reforms and leadership, Fullan (2004) asserted that capacity building gives leaders the ability to build future leaders through (a) maintaining and continuing to use their own professional development training and (b) focusing on both achievement and future development of school leaders. To explain these ideas, Fullan provided a successful example of capacity building in an innovative federally sponsored program titled School Teams Achieving Results for Students (STARS):

> In Chicago, people learn in weekly meetings, study groups, focused institutes, extended academies, and walkthrough site visits, during which teams visit schools to learn from and react to leadership and pedagogical strategies. STARS (School

Teams Achieving Results for Students), an innovative program launched with 135 schools in Chicago in 2002 and with 115 schools in Guilford County in 2003, focuses on building the capacity of school leadership teams to improve both pedagogy and results. This comprehensive, multiyear initiative includes school teacher-principal teams and district-level leaders in weeklong institutes and multiple-day follow-ups each year, thereby fostering deep professional learning communities across the districts. Cycles of application and regular examination of student results enhance the transfer of skills to classrooms and schools. (p. 44)

School Teams Achieving Results for Students

STARS projects are supported by federal grants. These grants serve as resources, bringing schools together for opportunities to talk one-on-one with state leaders. STARS give students the opportunity to take classes not offered in their own districts and to take virtual field trips. States are reaching for the same goals as STARS projects: to equalize education between rural and urban school districts and to serve the underserved population.

In studying the STARS, the researcher asked, What literature is presently in research that addresses an overall school district instructional technology planning for districts that may be suffering with the diffusion of large-scale instructional technology integration? In South Dakota, Simonson and Wheeler (2003) implemented a STARS school project for the state titled the Digital Dakota Network (DDN). The DDN is a statewide telecommunications network that connects 176 schools in South Dakota school districts. Simonson and Wheeler spearheaded a large-scale diffusion project that consisted of data that measured quantitative and qualitative components and summative and formative evaluation strategies that enabled researchers to evaluate the overall goals and objectives concerning the effectiveness of the DDN project:

> Formative evaluation made it possible for SDADE personnel to adjust aspects of the program as needed and addressed (1) the status of project objectives and (2) how activities have affected participants. Summative evaluation addressed the

overall effectiveness of the project and determined whether objectives have been met. (p. 12)

Some of the goals consisted of wiring all the schools, connecting the schools, and training the teachers. According to Simonson and Wheeler (2003), the academy titled Technology for Teaching and Learning was set up as an initiative mandated by former Governor Janklov to teach all instructors across the state how to integrate and use technology. The aim was for teachers to learn (a) to change teaching and learning in classrooms through the use of technology into the curriculum, (b) to model effective teaching practices using technology, and (c) to assist fellow educators in learning how to use technology.

Simonson and Wheeler (2003) noted that project results for the Technology for Teaching and Learning academies for teachers were as follows:

1. The need for additional training for teachers as an important factor for teachers using of DDN.

2. That visits to kindergarten through Grade 12 schools indicated the need for continuing professional development for success in kindergarten through Grade 12 school districts.

3. The need for continued support from administrators for teachers as a factor that contributed to the adoption of instructional technologies in kindergarten through Grade 12 classrooms.

Simonson and Wheeler (2003) explained how teachers and administrators worked together to ensure the success of the project:

> To encourage the use of the DDN in the classroom, administrators offered a half-day free time to teachers who were venturesome enough to attempt to integrate the DDN into their curriculum. Administrators were more than happy to cover a class for a teacher to use that time in developing new adaptations of the

technology for their students. (p. 19)

Again, what may be generalized from the data presented in the DDN project? Do certain patterns develop that school districts may examine to make concrete decisions regarding school leadership and the diffusion of instructional technology training? Are there regularities to assist leaders in schools with the huge amount of instructional technology diffusion?

Manternack and Muashak (1997) collected data during 1996 and 1997 for a final report on the STARS project of the Iowa Distance Education Alliance. The alliance included partnerships of Iowa's educational institutions that included the Iowa Department of Education, public television, 3 institutions, 15 community colleges, 15 area education agencies, and local education agencies. The purpose of the alliance was to implement a special statewide STARS school grant. The goals of the STARS schools project, according to Manternack and Muashak, were as follows:

1. To develop instructional materials for distance education.

2. To support the training and resources for distance education.

3. To provide training and technology support for distance education.

4. To extend information to the public about distance education.

5. To incorporate distance education in colleges and universities while involving teachers for future training.

6. To implement and integrate new technology in selected schools.

The grant has been instrumental in providing Iowa with the ability to implement and use fiber-optic technology for live, two-way, full-motion interactive instruction that has provided greater levels of interactivity than previous instructional technology has. Have the objectives and leadership been effectively planned for the adoption and diffusion of instructional technology in the Iowa STARS project, and what may be learned to aid in this applied study?

According to the report by Manternack and Muashak (1997), the use of classroom instructional technology has been identified and shared in the Iowa Communication Network database, and constant use of instructional technology by teachers has continued to grow. Moreover, the Iowa Communication Network has been used in classrooms for students in kindergarten through Grade 12 in the districts' schools. The project has integrated new educational approaches at the same time that new opportunities have been provided for underserved learners of all incomes including (a) limited-English proficient students, (b) Chapter 1 student minorities, and (c) students in rural schools. Courses have been offered that would not have been offered if the network were not in place.

The evidence indicated that goals and objectives of the Iowa STARS project were supported. Along with teacher training and support from leaders, the indicated changes have taken place in teacher behavior in using technology to enhance curricula and motivate students. The style of teachers' pedagogy has changed. Teachers (a) have been more geared toward student-centered instruction, a concept that has been integrated into other areas of curricula; (b) have been more focused on the content; (c) have recognized the advantages and disadvantages of using instructional technology and distance education; and (d) have experienced a sense of newness as they observed student interactions (Manternack & Muashak, 1997).

Although the diffusion process of instructional technology into the schools where this applied dissertation study took place looked at leadership and instructional technology in two school districts that were using instructional technology as a tool to enhance students' performance, the lack of resources for instructional technology training was also a focus. Clearly, the schools were equipped with instructional technology and equipment.

What may be generalized about leadership in any school districts that are diffused with instructional technology and struggling to maintain accreditation? What makes the difference in the schools that are equally diffused with instructional technology and have maintained accreditation? Using these questions, the researcher of this applied study attempted to look at patterns or regularities on which school leadership might base evidence to make sound decisions.

Significance of the Study

In a study of the characteristics of the leadership and the adoption of technology in schools, innovativeness may be approached in several ways. One approach is to look at organizations that generate passing scores on the state SOL assessment test and use the innovativeness of the individuals who possess characteristics associated with the opinion leadership characteristics as a guide. Another approach is to become accredited and to maintain accreditation by using the characteristics associated with the opinion leadership that may filter through school districts offering leadership training with ongoing strategic instruction technology planning for teachers. Educational leaders must understand that the adoption of technology is not the only piece in the puzzle of getting the full effect or credit for adoption (Rogers, 2003).

Nevertheless, why are some districts continuing to pass the state SOL assessment test, and how is full accreditation maintained? The answer to this question is significant. The results of this study might contribute to the answer and eventually might be very beneficial to the educational domain.

A lack of leadership and organizational innovativeness has contributed to teachers' poor instructional technology skills, as is clear in school districts that are not performing well on the state SOL assessment test. The lack of effective staff development sessions is one problem; an ineffective leadership strategy regarding the use of innovation in the organization is another.

Relationship of the Problem to the Literature

This review of related literature provided the researcher with insights concerning the Perceived Organizational Innovativeness Scale (PORGI), Individual Innovativeness (II) Scale, and a technology checklist for interviews. These instruments were designed to measure the instructional technology innovativeness of individual leaders and of the organization in schools that were meeting or failing to meet state accreditation standards. According to Hurt and Teigen (1977), "An innovation is an idea, practice, or object that is perceived as new by an individual or organization" (p. 377). The PORGI is used to measure how members of an organization perceive change. The research of Hurt and Teigen indicated that this orientation is associated with behavioral patterns.

The II Scale measures an individual's orientation toward change. Hurt, Joseph, and Cook (1977) noted that this orientation is associated with several communication variables and that the II Scale is highly reliable and has high predictive validity. The technology checklist consisting of open-ended interview questions generated data that measured any behavioral patterns that were associated with the use of instructional technology by leaders and their organizations and that led toward strategic growth, development, and training.

In this chapter, the researcher identified the three constructs that were explored in this study. These constructs were as follows: (a) The innovativeness construct that measured the attitudes toward innovativeness of individual leaders and the organizational innovativeness; (b) the performance construct that measured the performance of schools that were passing and failing state accreditation standards; and (c) a technology checklist that measured strategies often used by leaders to promote instructional technology strategies for individual growth, development, and training.

Exploring the work of Fullan, Bertani, and Quinn (2004) led the researcher to ask, As innovativeness increases, do performance and instructional technology integration and strategies by the individuals (leaders) and the organization also increase? And if they do, are the attitudes toward innovativeness of leaders and the organization's innovativeness responsible for the individual's innovativeness (instructional technology) that increases performance in schools passing standards of accreditation? Beyond the discussion of these instruments, this researcher pinpointed accountability as a factor in an organization's performance and on the impact of NCLB mandates (Dillon, 2006).

Further, this researcher explored the innovation decision process and the relationship to individual innovativeness adoption categories and discussed organization and individual innovativeness, highlighting organizational leadership and teachers' use of instructional technology (Barnett, 2001; Feldner & Kincaid, 2002). The term *performance* has been defined for this study as passing scores mandated by NCLB and enforced by a state department of education. Performance data indicated whether schools in a district passed the SOL assessment test and whether, as a result, full accreditation was gained for all schools in the district (Phillips, 2006; Wepner, 2006).

Accreditation Process

The term *accreditation*, for the purpose of this study, refers to the process used by a state department of education to evaluate a district's educational performance according to state regulations. In this section, the researcher examined the process in school districts located in the southeastern sector of the United States. Every school year, the state education department personnel review the regulations to establish a blueprint for the next school year. On May 24, 2006, the state board of education for both the inner-city and the suburban districts approved and adopted the regulations establishing the SOL. This approval also established the standards of accreditation for public schools.

Requirements for Graduation. For students entering the ninth grade, the requirements for a diploma are as follows:

1. Students should have completed all courses successfully to be offered credits before reaching Grade 9.

2. Students in Grades 9 through 12 will receive credit toward standard units required for graduation if the courses meet the SOL's content requirement or are equal in content and academic requirements at the secondary level. To earn a verified credit, a student must meet the state requirements by passing eight verified credits (see Appendixes A and B).

Accreditation Status. Schools that achieve full accreditation status are eligible for the Governor's Award for Outstanding Achievement. Districts that are fully accredited show significant signs of improvement in student performance. High schools and middle schools are fully accredited when students achieve passing rates of 70% or above in four content areas. A combination of a passing rate of at least 75% on English tests in Grades 3 and 5 is required for accreditation at an elementary school (Virginia Department of Education, 2006a).

Any school district that raises a rating of accreditation with warning to full accreditation in a year receives the Governor's Award for Outstanding Achievement. District schools that are denied accreditation are subject to sanction by the state board of education. Schools that are not accredited must prepare a report detailing ways in which the school plans to take corrective action and to implement those actions. The report must be signed by the school principal, division superintendent, and local school board chair (Virginia Department of Education, 2006a). Further, within 30 days of receiving notice of accreditation status, nonaccredited schools have to provide to all of the students' parents written notification of the school's accreditation status and the plan of action to correct the deficiencies.

Accountability and Leadership

One factor that remains dominant is making sure that individuals are held accountable for students' performance, as spelled out by the goals and visions of an organization. As Dahir and Stone (2003) wrote, "Accountability requires systematically collecting, analyzing, and using critical data elements to understand the current achievements . . . for students, and to begin to strategize, impact, and document how the school . . . program contributes toward supporting student success" (p. 214).

State departments of education are responsible for quick changes to the organization, changes that bring about school reforms, changes, and accountability issues (Dikkers et al., 2005). Kelly (as cited in Soars & Soars, 2002) found that further changes are being channeled to many of the school agencies in the hope of combining and consolidating powers with legislators to impress voters.

As a result, states have locked in any previous power achieved by legislative initiatives (Wepner, 2006). Wepner noted that students are not being held accountable for low performance and actually are less accountable than leaders in the organization. In light of this, leaders are continuing to struggle to figure out what will work without damaging students or jeopardizing current positions.

Ross, McGraw, and Burdett (2001) found that many districts are involved in initiatives that support instructional technology. As evidence grows concerning the impact that instructional technology has on curricula, the demand for it is increasing. Evaluation and assessment go hand in hand with school accountability.

In this study, the term *assessment* refers to the performance of a school district in relation to a district's passing or failing performance on state standards of accreditation, and the use of instructional technologies by school leaders. The term *evaluation* refers to the measurement of the innovativeness of the school leaders, and the school divisions, depending (a) on the degree of effectiveness of the use of strategies associated with the innovation across the school district and (b) on the degree of effectiveness of the innovation in the school curricula (Adams, 2006).

Ross et al. (2001) indicated that Rockman believed that the need to evaluate the school district and derive positive assessment strategies is based on a school district's innovative strategies, and how effectively that innovation relates to the overall goals of the school district. Few leaders lack skills to be good evaluators. But instructional technology has resulted in increased pressure on the leaders in a district. Ross et al. indicated that, for technology to have a positive impact on performance achievement of students, educational leaders must envision, direct, and support the successful diffusion of innovation integration of instructional technology into teaching, learning and school management.

Diffusion Theory and Instructional Technology

Diffusion definition. Rogers (2003) defined the term *diffusion* as "the process in which an innovation is communicated through certain channels over time among members of a social system" (p. 5). From another perspective, the school district acts as a change agent who seeks to persuade an individual or a school division to adopt an innovation.

Relationship of diffusion theory and instructional technology. Instructional technology has suffered in some school districts from lack of use. Researchers have focused on the diffusion theory in an attempt to increase the adoption of instructional technologies in school districts (LaRose & Hoag, 1996; Surry, 1997). Four factors are involved in the diffusion process: the innovation itself, communication, time, and the social system (Rogers, 2003). These factors have been shown to influence the implementation and innovativeness of an individual and the school district.

Researchers have shown that the diffusion theory is valuable in instructional technology and have explained why some innovations are not adopted. According to Surry (1997), the number of reasons for the lack of use of instructional technology is as numerous as the number of instructional technologies. Some of the reasons for the lack of use include leaders' resistance to change, deeply rooted bureaucracies, and funding issues (Flannery, 2006). Surry asserted that the diffusion theory is not only a well-defined and unified theory but also involves a large number of theories focusing on the innovation process.

Innovation Decision Process

During the innovation decision process, the individual or school district acquires and acts on knowledge about an innovation. Then, a period follows that involves the formulation of an attitude toward the innovation. Finally, the period of decision arrives, when leaders must adopt or reject the innovation, and, if they adopt it, they must implement and confirm it (Rogers, 2003).

Researchers have supported the innovation decision process, an approach that is widely cited in the instructional technology literature (Surry, 1997). For instance, Surry quoted Sachs as stating the following:

> After looking at [the literature] in our field, one might get the impression that the only important thing we need to know about is how to encourage the adoption of innovations the change agents, and the five stages of the innovation adoption process (Innovation Decision Process, ¶ 9).

Although Sachs noted that other theories have been overlooked, the innovation decision process is by far the most widely used and well known.

Individuals' Innovativeness and School Districts' Innovativeness

Surrey (1997) found that individuals and school districts that have considered innovativeness will adopt an innovation much earlier than less predisposed individuals. In clarifying the term *school district*, Rogers (2003) defined it as "a system of individuals who work together to achieve common goals through a hierarchy of ranks and a division of labor" (p. 404). The structure of the school districts, Rogers added, is created to carry out large-scale tasks. Surprisingly enough, Rogers found that the data acquired in studies were from an individual in a school district such as the superintendent of the school district or designated central office appointee.

According to Rogers (2003), the school district is usually treated as a single entity when being analyzed. The innovativeness of school districts has been widely studied. Hundreds of studies of school districts' innovativeness were completed by the 1970s. Moreover, research on diffusion in the school district focused on the innovativeness process as opposed to the innovativeness of the district. These variables of innovativeness emphasized the decision process of the individual innovation. Rogers wrote that the larger the school district, the more innovative it is.

Using the following example, Rogers (2003) illustrated equivalence between the independent and the dependent variables. In school districts, studies have found little relationship between data representing independent variables that measure qualities of a school district and data representing dependent variables that measure innovativeness of a school district quantifiably as a composite score. One problem that Rogers has gleaned on the relationship of the independent variable and the dependent variable is that only top officials provide the data that represent the entire school district. This approach to data collection gives inadequate representation of the true behavior of an entire school district.

This approach to data was not used in this applied dissertation study. This researcher did not set the boundaries of data collection solely on the organization's innovativeness, but expanded the boundaries to include the innovativeness of individuals in the organization. According to Rogers (2003), "Gathering data only from a few individuals at the top of a large sample of a school district does not seem to prove very valid measures of the concepts of study" (p. 409). In general, Rogers concluded, "[The size of a school district] has consistently been found to be positively related to its innovativeness . . . and, therefore, it can be generalized that larger school districts are more innovative" (p. 409).

Innovativeness Adoption Categories

Although individuals in any school district may adopt innovation, do these individuals adopt the innovations at the same time? According to Rogers (2003), the answer is no. Based on this answer, researchers may classify innovators by categories. Individuals or school districts are categorized according to characteristics associated with the innovativeness if the individual and school district. The classification of individuals using the category process is beneficial. A researcher may group individuals according to characteristics of the innovativeness of individuals or of districts.

The time of adoption is used in much research and is a highly used variable that establishes a sequence, according to the adoption of an innovation by the individual or the school district. Rogers (2003) found that the adoption of an innovation follows a normal, bell-shaped curve when plotted over time on a frequency basis. If the cumulative members of the adopter category are plotted, the result is an S-shaped curve (see Appendix C).

Because the normal frequency distributions of the S-shaped curve have been characterized, researchers have been able to categorize the adoption of an innovation. Using the mean to measure the averages of individuals, the standard deviation measures the variation of the mean score, or how far individuals and the school district are from the mean, based on innovativeness. This process of mean interpretation, according to Rogers (2003), is used to divide a normal adoption distribution into five categories. A description of the application of these five categories to school faculty is provided in the following section.

Applying Rogers' Five Categories to School Faculty

Rogers (2003) developed and Marinho (2003) described how faculty members use the following five categories: innovators, early adopters, early majority, late majority, and laggards. These categories of school faculty are explained as follows:

1. Innovators are characterized by venturesome leadership. New ideas lead them out of a circle of peer networks and into more cosmopolitan relationships. Innovators exhibit (a) control of substantial financial resources, (b) the ability to understand and apply complex technical knowledge, (c) the ability to cope with a high degree of uncertainty about an innovation at the time they adopt it, (d) a willingness to accept an occasional setback when a new idea proves unsuccessful as inevitably happens, and (e) the ability to play a gatekeeping role in regard to the flow of new ideas into a system.

2. Early adopters have respected leadership characteristics. They are a more integrated part of the local social system than are innovators. Early adopters have the highest degree of opinion leadership in most systems. They are considered by many to be the individual with whom to check before adopting a new idea, and they are generally sought by change agents as a local missionary for speeding the diffusion process. Early adopters (a) are respected by their peers; (b) know that, to continue to earn this esteem of colleagues and to maintain a central position in the communication networks of the system, they must make judicious innovation decisions; (c) decrease uncertainty about a new idea by adopting it; (d) convey a subjective evaluation of the innovation to near peers through interpersonal networks; and (e) put their stamp of approval on a new idea by adopting it.

3. Early majority people exhibit deliberate leadership characteristics. They adopt a new idea just before the average member of a system. Early majority people interact frequently with their peers but seldom hold positions of opinion leadership in a system. Early majority people (a) are in a unique location between the very early and relatively late adopters and are, therefore, an important link in the diffusion process; (b) provide interconnectedness in the system's interpersonal networks; (c) are members of one of the most numerous adopter categories, making up a third of all members of a system; and (d) have a decision period for an innovation longer than that of innovators and early adopters.

4. Late majority people are skeptical. They adopt new ideas just after the average member of a system. Like the early majority, the late majority make up a third of the members of a system. Late majority people (a) approach innovations with a skeptical and cautious mind, (b) do not adopt until most others in their system have already done so,

and (c) require the pressure of peers to motivate adoption. Most of the uncertainty about a new idea must be removed before late majority people feel safe to adopt the new idea.

5. Laggards are the last in a social system to adopt an innovation. They possess almost no opinion leadership. Laggards are the most localized of all adopter categories in their outlook. Laggards (a) often base decisions on what has been done previously; (b) interact primarily with others who also have relatively traditional values; (c) tend to be suspicious of innovations and of change agents; (d) have a relatively lengthy decision process for innovation, with adoption and use falling far behind awareness of a new idea; and (e) have limited resources and must be certain that a new idea will not fail before they adopt it. A precarious economic position often forces the laggard to be extremely cautious in adopting innovations.

Leadership

Popham (2000) referred to leaders as educators who are responsible for influencing colleagues, who have an impact on students, and who are bound by those responsibilities. For the purpose of this study, leaders are school districts with leaders who influence the attitude and behaviors of individuals (teachers) informally with relative frequency. These leaders hold a position that is informal and usually is earned through technical competence, social accessibility, and the leader's conformity to the school districts' norms (Rogers, 2003). Leadership in the organization has been the focus of school reform since the NCLB legislation (Sunderman, Orfield, & Kim, 2006; Tetreaut, 2005). Given the trend toward quantifying school progress, accountability, and student performance, Lambert (2004) contended that consideration should be given to all variables involving the progress or failure associated with the school environment.

The emergence of advanced instructional technology, coupled with outcomes that are measured by accountability, has led to an enormous amount of research on leadership and the impact it has on a school district (Leithwood & Reihl, 2003). Research provides good evidence that supports quality leadership in a school district as a key to improving the motivation of teachers and the adoption of instructional technology by school leaders. According to Leithwood and Riehl, a wealth of evidence suggests that the quality of leadership positively enhances teaching and learning. Leadership has been shown to make a difference to a school's ability to improve by influencing the motivation of teachers and the quality of teaching that takes place in the classroom. Ultimately, it influences whether a school is likely to succeed or fail against the odds.

Leithwood and Reihl (2003) noted that large-scale studies of schooling conclude that the effects of leadership on student learning are small but educationally significant. School leadership, therefore, matters; however, the degree to which it matters remains a contentious issue.

Leadership of principals, supervisors, and instructors is necessary to support and implement educational change (Lambert, 2004). Early researchers referred to the pros and cons of leadership, but what does more current research say about the behavior of leaders and the characteristics that individuals must possess to adopt and implement educational strategies?

In a survey of American teachers conducted by MetLife (Virginia Education Association, 2005), data were collected from teachers and principals in response to questions about leadership and its relationship to the adoption of an innovation. The results showed that the groups gave different responses concerning the adoption of an innovation by leaders and the impact of the adoption in reference to the innovation and to the leader's ability to motivate teachers, their satisfaction, and their commitment.

In a study conducted by Lambert (2004) on the qualities of servant leadership, the data indicated a significant relationship between a principal's leadership and adoption of innovation and school achievement. The results of research conducted by Marzano, McNulty, and Walters (2004) supported Lambert conclusion that effective leadership substantially improves student achievement.

Opinion leaders. The degree to which a leader is able to consistently influence his or her coworkers' attitudes or behaviors determines whether he or she is an opinion leader. According to Rogers (2003), the behavior of leaders in the educational environment is important when a school district is adopting innovations. Furthermore, school leaders who are comfortable with technological innovations often influence the behavior of coworkers (Copeland & Gray, 2002). Change agents in a school district link the behavior of the opinion leaders directly to success (Rogers).

Change agents. Change agents provide the communication link between resources (instructional technology) and the teachers in the school district (Clarke, 1991; Ruebling et al., 2004). In this study, the term *change agent* refers to leaders in the district (technology coordinators) who are required by a state department of education to have a degree in a specialized area. The change agents may be instrumental to an opinion leader. The relationship of the opinion leaders and the change agents may develop into a strategy that promotes long-term job security for employees, consensus decision making, and slow evaluation (on-the-job performance). The trend is to shift coworkers and opinion leaders from dependence on change agents to self-reliance (Rogers, 2003).

Reasons Teachers Use Instructional Technology

Instructional technology definition. According to Seels and Richey (1994), the term *instructional technology* is "the theory and practice of design, development, utilization, management, and evaluation of process and resources for learning" (p. 10). For the sake of this study, instructional technology is defined as technology adopted by the school district and used by individuals for the sole purpose of improving the school learning systems (Meghabghab & Price, 1997). The goal of instructional technology training for classroom teachers is to provide them with the tools to help students improve their academic performance (Marzano et al., 2004). According to Abrams and Lock (2001), teachers use instructional technology as a tool to enhance and improve the learning process.

Instructional technology use in classrooms. Leadership that promotes instructional technology in the classroom is a key ingredient to improving student learning (Ruebling et al., 2004). Examinations of the literature concerning the value of instructional technology in the classroom have demonstrated that school leaders are aware of the potential that instructional technology has for enhancing students' performance (Buck & Horton, 1996).

Further research has demonstrated that leaders should not be isolated from instructional technology and should be involved in the decision-making process for adopting it (Grimes, 2005; Marinho, 2003). The human factor in the decision to implement instructional technology programs is the reason given in some organizations for leaders to support technology in the classroom (Rogers, 2003; Shuldman, 2004).

Raising Teachers' Motivation When Integrating Instructional Technology

In the first decade of the 21st century, many school districts are struggling with the newer approaches. Students need new avenues and skills to integrate into their communities with the necessary computer skills to compete in the job market (Consortium for School Networking, 2004). Leaders have the responsibility of ensuring that all students have an opportunity to explore basic computer skills and use instructional technology in an effort to assist schools to maintain accreditation on state assessment standards (Voogt, Moonrn, Akker, & Almekinders, 2005).

Raising leadership abilities and comfort levels in using instructional technology is easier when the school leaders' support for teachers is adequate. Findings indicated that the greater the support and practical experiences that teachers have, the greater the commitment, motivation, and satisfaction with instructional technology (Casey & Rakes, 2002b). Leaders in an educational organization must realize that adoption of innovation brings about change, and different pedagogical methods encourage better leadership in an educational organization (Fullan et al., 2004). One of the biggest obstacles to the use of instructional technology in an educational organization is the lack of support for leadership (Dooley, 1999).

Shuldman (2004) examined the findings of three superintendents in a New Hampshire school district and found that some teachers were not using instructional technology. The study indicated that lack of commitment, low levels of motivation, and lack of leadership support from leaders impeded the process. Shengold and Hadley (as cited in Casey & Rakes, 2002a) pointed to the failure of leaders to motivate and involve teachers in the decision-making process. They also suggested that teachers who use appropriate instructional technology do so because they are involved in the decision-making process, are supported by educational leaders, are satisfied and motivated, and are committed to their leaders.

Summary

To measure the innovativeness of an organization, the PORGI has been used in many studies. To measure the innovativeness of individuals, the II Scale has been used in many studies. Writers of related literature noted that, when individuals and organizations adopt instructional technology, they have used both of these scales to measure the basic characteristics associated with organization innovativeness and individual innovativeness. Rogers (2003) associated these characteristics with adopter categories. The categories, when plotted, follow a normal bell curve. When represented by cumulative data of frequency over time, the curve becomes S-shaped (see Appendix C). The characteristics of an individual and an organization may be divided into a normal distribution of five categories: innovators, early adopters, early majority, late majority, and laggards.

In this study, the category into which the inner-city and the suburban districts fell was key to determining the characteristics associated with each district and each school passing the SOL assessment. Researchers supported the need for leadership to be evaluated for school accountability and student performance. Quality leadership improves teachers' motivation and their use of instructional technology. A wealth of research evidence has indicated the quality of leadership as a key factor. For instance, Lambert (2004) found that a relationship exists between school leadership and the adoption of innovation and school achievement. Moreover, the findings of Marzano et al. (2004) supported those of Lambert: Effective leadership substantially improves student achievement, and the opinion of leaders does have a profound effect on performance. When leaders support teachers using instructional technology, teachers have greater motivation, commitment, and satisfaction (Casey & Rakes, 2002b; Finegan, Shamian, Spencer-Laschinger, & Wilk, 2004). The role of change agents (technology coordinators) and opinion leaders (principals) is of great significance for an organization's resources for their communicating over time about the adoption of an innovation into school districts, resources that include both teachers and change agents.

Chapter 3: Methodology

Overview

In this chapter, the research design, participants, instruments, research variables, and implementation procedures are explained. The design and method of this study were challenging in all phases, from the collection of data to the analysis of data, the recruitment of participants, and the use of regular mail.

Participants

This study had three phases. The first involved a stratification sample consisting of interviews involving 9 principals. The participating schools included three elementary schools, three middle schools, and three high schools. The criteria for selecting each school principal for interview sessions involved the school's pass-fail score on the SOL assessment: Two principals had to lead schools that have scored a passing grade on the state SOL assessment test and passed accreditation, and two principals had to lead schools that have failed the SOL assessment test and be on probation or without accreditation.

Next, 40 schools and 200 principals were invited to participate in the study. The demographics of the schools were not a part of the screening; nevertheless, principals of all three levels of district schools (elementary, middle, and high school) participated. A total of 184 principals responded to the PORGI for both districts. A total of 193 principals responded to the II Scale. The combined participation rate of 94% was a justifiable rate for interpreting the data results.

The study lasted for a period of 3 to 4 months. The researcher examined the records of district schools that passed and that failed accreditation standards. District leaders from the central office were asked to nominate administrators and schools to take part in the study based on each school's performance on accreditation standards.

Principals were nominated regardless of years of experience, school demographics, strategic development, growth or training of instructional technology.

The two school districts are located within a mile of each other. The inner-city district has continued to struggle to maintain passing performance scores and full accreditation for the SOL assessments. The suburban district has shown remarkable and consistent improvement in SOL and has demonstrated full accreditation and passing performance scores. Both districts are equipped with Internet capabilities including wireless and a local area network. The suburban district has been well known for good leadership and academic performance on SOL assessments. The inner-city district has struggled with maintaining the state standards performance criteria mandated by the state accreditation policy. Both groups share similar characteristics, as defined by the state department of education that sets the guidelines and criteria for hiring persons for administrative positions.

Participants were familiar with the overall goals and visions pertaining to instructional technology development and training that were defended by the district school board. In fact, the inner-city district requires that all employees sign a contract that they understand that instructional technology training and development are mandated. In the researcher's judgment, whether the goals and visions for instructional technology are implemented or enforced by leaders in both districts needed to be investigated further.

Purpose of Project

The purpose of this concurrent, mixed-method study was to investigate the phenomena associated with the characteristics of the innovativeness and the overall performance of the two school districts. A secondary purpose was to investigate the phenomena associated with certain characteristics of leaders and leaders' perceptions of school innovativeness and performance. Another purpose was to investigate the use of instructional technology strategies used by school district leaders for growth, development, and training.

Research Questions

The following research questions guided the study:

1. What are the innovativeness characteristics of leadership in schools that have demonstrated passing performance on SOL tests?

2. What are the innovativeness characteristics of the organization passing state accreditation performance?

3. How often is professional staff involved in instructional technology training?

4. What strategies are implemented by organizational leaders for growth, development, and training?

5. How are strategies for instructional technology adoption and integration implemented?

Instruments

Phase 1: PORGI. Quantitatively, the PORGI measures how members of an organization perceive change (see Appendix D). Research conducted by Hurt and Teigen (1977) indicated that this orientation is associated with behavioral patterns. PORGI has been used many times in the studies and has an alpha reliability above .90 and a very good predictive validity. The scale has 25 items. Subjects respond to each item using a 5-point Likert scale that ranged from *strongly disagree* to *strongly agree*.

Phase 2: II Scale. Quantitatively, the II Scale measures an individual's orientation towards change (see Appendix E). Research by Hurt et al. (1977) indicated that this orientation is associated with several communication variables and that it is highly reliable and has high predictive validity. The scale has 20 items. Subjects respond to each item using a 5-point Likert scale that ranged from *strongly disagree* to *strongly agree*.

Phase 3: Interview instrument. Twelve principals were interviewed. Each interview lasted 10 to 20 minutes. Each principal responded to a 4-point Likert scale that ranged from *strongly disagree* to *strongly agree*. The scale consisted of 15 questions (see Appendix F). A logbook was used for tracking interview responses. Demographics included each principal's school level, years of experience, and the school's pass-fail status (see Appendix G).

Procedure

For confidentiality purposes, the researcher maintained all data in a locked filing cabinet. The use of consent forms was not applicable to participants in this study. The researcher distributed the two survey instruments that were completed anonymously to each school involved in the study by regular mail, school mail, and hand delivery at a faculty meeting. A list of all participating schools' addresses was gathered using the district's Web site. Participants were asked to respond to two surveys administered at different times.

All interviewed principals agreed to participate in the phone interviews and received explicit details about the study and the procedures governing the process. Nine principals were interviewed, and all responses from the 9 principals were included in this study.

The study began in early spring of 2007 when the PORGI was distributed. The II Scale was distributed in late spring 2007. The survey instruments had detailed instructions, confidentiality was noted, and procedures were explained for returning the instruments. Time estimate for completion of surveys was 20 to 30 minutes per survey.

For nonrespondents, a second attempt was made in the fall of 2007 inviting persons to complete both survey instruments.

Interviews were conducted in the summer by telephone and the sample consisted of 9 participants who were interviewed for 10 to 20 minutes. The interview consisted of 15 questions. Each question related to strategies often used by leaders to promote instructional technology strategies for individual growth, development, and training (Tomei, 2002). The summer months were chosen for interviews because the administrators were available with very little distraction.

Data Analysis

Descriptive statistical analyses were performed for responses to each research question. Measures of central tendency (means, medians, and other percentiles) and dispersion (standard deviations, ranges) were computed, and frequency distributions were analyzed. In addition, descriptive statistical analysis of the responses to the interview focused on the taxonomy of 15 instructional technology questions that were recorded and based on a 4-point Likert scale with the following ratings: 1 = *strongly agree*, 2 = *undecided*, 3 = *agree*, and 4 = *strongly agree*. The results were correlated according to frequency percentages for responses.

Summary

The methodology for this applied research involved conducting the study distributing instruments and information by regular mail and school mail, hand delivery at a faculty meeting, and telephone communication. Participants responded anonymously. Individuals and the organization responded to two surveys regarding the innovativeness of an individual and the organization. The design focused on a leadership model that drew on several phenomenological factors. In the researcher's judgment, if the analyses from the descriptive statistics results and from the quantitative strategies for acquiring data were successful, then several generalizations would be made about behavioral patterns associated with strategies that relate to instructional technology planning by school leaders.

Chapter 4: Results

The chief purpose of this study was to examine the phenomena associated with the characteristics of each of the two school district's innovativeness and the overall performance of each of the school districts. A secondary purpose was to investigate the phenomena associated with certain characteristics of leaders and leaders' the perceptions of school district innovativeness and school district performance. Last, this study investigated the use of instructional technology strategies used by school district leaders for growth, development, and training. The research questions tested in this study were as follows:

1. What are the innovativeness characteristics of leadership in schools that have demonstrated passing performance on SOL tests?

2. What are the innovativeness characteristics of the organization passing the state's accreditation performance?

3. How often are professional staff members involved in instructional technology training?

4. What strategies are identified to be implemented by organizational leaders for growth, development, and training?

5. How are strategies for instructional technology adoption and integration implemented?

In this chapter, the researcher explained the results in demographic profiles of the sample studied, both descriptive and inferential results for each research hypothesis and findings that supported the research questions. All tests were conducted at the .05 level of significance.

Demographic Profiles

Data for this descriptive research design were collected from the principals of schools in two districts using the PORGI and the Interview Technology Checklist instruments. The PORGI measured organizational innovativeness and the Interview Technology Checklist measured the strategies used by leaders. The researcher analyzed the demographic data of the sample's performance accreditation (see Tables 1 and 2). The findings for the demographic data indicated that, of the 113 schools sampled from the two districts, 63.6% were elementary schools, 17.7% were middle schools, and 18.6% were high schools.

Table 1

Performance Accreditation of Schools in the Suburban District, by Number

School	Passing	Failing
High school	8	2
Middle school	9	2
Elementary school	42	0

Table 2

Performance Accreditation of Schools in the Inner-City District, by Number

School	Passing	Failing
High school	11	0
Middle school	6	3
Elementary school	28	2

The researcher also analyzed the frequencies of responses to the PORGI and II Scale concerning the individual and organizational innovativeness characteristics of leadership in the schools sampled from the inner-city district, responses that described the perceived disposition of the participants toward new technology. Organizational innovativeness measures identified leadership as mostly displaying the characteristics of early adopters of new technology, whereas individual innovativeness measures identified leadership as chiefly displaying the characteristics of the early majority.

A small percentage of responses were for leadership as innovators from organizational (3.2%) and from individual innovativeness (3.2%) measures. However, the researcher found that, (a) for leadership perceived as early adopters, 23.7% responded individual and 63.4% responded organizational innovativeness; (b) as early majority, 39.8% showed individual and 25.8% showed organizational innovativeness; (c) as late majority, 26.9% showed for individual and 7.5% showed organizational innovativeness; and (d) as laggards, only 6.5% showed individual innovativeness (see Table 3).

Table 3

Participants' Perceptions of Individual and Organization Innovativeness in the Inner-City District, by Number

Variables	Individual	Organization
Innovators	3	3
Early adopters	22	59
Early majority	37	24
Late majority	25	7
Laggards	6	0

The researcher also analyzed the findings for the frequencies of responses to the

PORGI and II Scale, concerning the individual and organizational innovativeness characteristics of leadership in the schools sampled from the suburban district, responses that described the perceived disposition of the participants toward new technology. Organizational innovativeness measures identified leadership as mostly displaying early adopters of new technology, whereas individual innovativeness measures identified leadership as mostly displaying early majority.

Percentage responses were found for leadership perceived as innovators from organizational (7%) and from individual innovativeness (3.3%) measures. In addition, for leadership perceived (a) as early adopters, 14% showed individual and 46.2% showed organizational innovativeness; (b) as early majority, 45% showed individual and 41.8% showed organizational innovativeness; (c) as late majority, 30% showed individual and 8.8% showed organizational innovativeness; and (d) as laggards, 7% showed individual innovativeness with none showing organizational innovativeness (see Table 4).

Table 4

Participants' Perceptions of Individual and Organization Innovativeness in the Suburban District, by Number

Variables	Individual	Organization
Innovators	7	3
Early adopters	14	42
Early majority	45	38
Late majority	30	8
Laggards	7	0

Descriptive Statistics

Participants were asked to respond to questions regarding the PORGI and II Scale. This was in response to the innovativeness characteristics of leadership in schools that demonstrated a passing performance on SOL test. The findings in Table 5 indicated that, on average, the PORGI scores were higher than II Scale scores and that the inner-city district scores were slighter higher than those of the suburban district. Results from passing performance as measured by the SOL test showed that the mean rating was slightly higher for the suburban district's passing performance ($M = 0.7204$; $SD = 0.539$; $N = 63$) than for that of the inner-city district ($M = 0.6129$; $SD = 0.609$; $N = 50$).

Table 5

Descriptive Statistics for Measures of Innovativeness

Measure	N	Min	Max	M	SD
		Inner-city district			
Individual Innovativeness Scale	93	45	92	60.78	10.25
Perceived Organizational Innovativeness Scale	93	54	124	92.76	12.69
		Suburban district			
Individual Innovativeness Scale	100	45	90	59.91	10.08
Perceived Organizational Innovativeness Scale	91	54	124	88.40	13.32

Note. N = valid N; Min = minimum; Max = maximum.

For further analysis, the researcher used the Pearson's correlation coefficient test to measure the relationship between the measures taken from the PORGI and II Scale instruments. Pearson's product moment correlation coefficient is most commonly used to measure a relationship between two variables, may be any value between -1 and 1, and is most accurate when the variable measures show sufficient covariance (a statistic representing the degree to which two variables vary together). This statistic indicates the strength and direction of the relationship.

The findings from the correlational analysis showed that the suburban district had significant positive correlations between individual innovativeness and organizational innovativeness for all categories for perceived disposition toward new technology (see Table 6). These results suggested that the more innovative the organization, the more likely the individual will exhibit innovativeness toward new technology.

Table 6

Pearson's Correlation Statistics of Measures From the PORGI and II Scales for Two Districts

Variables	Inner-city	Suburban
Innovators	.095	.203
Early adopters	.741	.865
Early majority	-.595	.650
Late majority	-.330	.438
Laggards	--	--

Note. PORGI = Perceived Organizational Innovativeness Scale; II = Individual Innovativeness; -- = no correlation because at least one variable was constant; inner-city early adopters and suburban innovators = significant relationship at $p < 0.05$ (2-tailed); inner-city early and late majorities and suburban early adopters and early and late majorities = significant relationship at $p < 0.01$ (2-tailed).

The findings from the correlation analysis showed that the suburban district had significant positive correlations between individual innovativeness and organizational innovativeness for all categories for perceived disposition toward new technology. These results indicated that the more innovative the organization, the more likely the individual will exhibit innovativeness toward new technology.

For the inner-city district, the results revealed a significant positive correlation between individual innovativeness and organizational innovativeness for early adopters; however, a significant negative correlation existed between individual innovativeness and organizational innovativeness for the early and late majority. These findings indicated that the more innovative the organization, the less likely the individual will show innovativeness at these scale levels. Scores for early and late majority ranged from 46 to 68 for individual innovativeness and from 50 to 90 for organizational innovativeness. Scores of 50 and below (laggards) resulted in constant variable scores of zero. A zero is a positive indication that similarities of adoption characteristics exist among schools according to the five categories of adoption and the diffusion theory.

Interview Findings

For clarity, nine interviews were conducted, or a 100% participation rate. The technology checklist consisted of 15 questions, but only 14 questions were used to measure patterns and frequencies of behavior in the same categories for schools that employed instructional technology for strategic growth, development, and training. Participants responded to a 4-point Likert scale with ratings that ranged from *strongly disagree* to *strongly agree*. Phenomena identified by responses that predominantly agreed or strongly agreed with the statements were the ratings concerning the computers in the school building with respect to their age and whether they had CD-ROM capabilities and access to the Internet and printers. Respondents agreed, to some extent, that the computer software reflected the curricula as required by the SOL: Findings for the interview questionnaire showed that 4.5% of the respondents strongly disagreed; 20.5% disagreed; 31.1% agreed, and 43.9% strongly agreed.

Findings Across All Interviewed Participants

Findings for Research Questions 3 through 5 were analyzed. Interview Questions 1 through 10 examined the instructional technology used in the building. The responses of the participants were *undecided*, resulting in a frequency of 4 participants, or a cumulative percentage of 44.4 of participants whose scores were similar and who had the same response. The data indicated that most were undecided about the amount of instructional technology used in the building. This response supported the action of considering the concerns of teachers in decision making when implementing an instructional technology program. Furthermore, the results were clearly an indication concerning the reason leaders who supported the use of instructional technology should not be isolated from the concerns of teachers and from the implementation and adoption process.

Interview Question 1 examined the use of instructional technology for classroom grading. The responses of the participants were *strongly disagree,* resulting in a frequency of 2 and 4 who were *undecided* and accounted for a cumulative percentage of 66.6 of participants whose scores were similar and who decided on the same response (see Table 7). Interview Question 2 examined the use of instructional technology with lesson plans. The results from participants were *agree* and *strongly agree* and accounted for a cumulative percentage of 77.8 of participants whose scores were similar and who had the same response. Interview Question 3 examined the use of instructional technology for out-of-class assignments. It resulted in a frequency equivalent of 3 participants, between *strongly disagree* and *undecided*, with a percentage of 33.3%, and *agree* with a cumulative percentage of 55.5.

Table 7

Participants' Responses to Interview Technology Checklist, by Number

Variable	SD	U	A	SA
Areas of teachers' use of instructional technology				
1. Grading.	2	4	--	2
2. Lesson preparation.	--	1	4	3
3. Out-of-class assignments.	1	2	4	1
4. Professional development.	--	3	3	2
5. Curricula are integrated.	--	2	5	2
6. Reflects SOL curricula.	--	2	3	4
7. Computer software is available and based on teachers' input.	--	3	3	3
8. Initial training of instructional technology is over 6 months old.	1	3	3	2
9. Initial training of instructional technology in last 6 months.	1	5	2	1
10. Training available on demand and monitored by the principal.	1	2	3	3
Ratings for computers in school building				
11. Less than 3 years old.	--	--	3	6
12. CD-ROM capable.	--	--	2	7
13. Most are connected to the Internet.	--	--	2	7
14. Most are connected to a printer.	--	--	4	5

Note. $N = 9$; ratings: SD = *strongly disagree*; U = *undecided*; A = *agree*; SA = *strongly agree*; -- = 0.

Interview Question 4 examined the use of instructional technology for professional development. It resulted in a frequency equivalent of 3 participants responding *agree*, 2 participants responded *strongly agree*, and a cumulative percentage of 66.7 of participants who responded *agree* or *strongly agree*. *Undecided* accounted for the remaining 33.3%. Interview Question 5 examined the integration of instructional technology with curricula. The responses from 5 participants were *agree*, with a cumulative percentage of 77.8 of participants who responded *agree* and *strongly agree*.

Interview Question 6 examined the use of technology for SOL curricula. It resulted in a frequency equivalent of 4 participants responding *strongly agree* and 3 participants responding *agree*, with a cumulative percentage of 77.8. For Interview Question 7, computer software adoption involving input from teachers resulted in a frequency equivalent of 3 participants for *undecided* with a cumulative percentage of 66.7 for *agree* and *strongly agree*. Interview Question 7 examined instructional technology software being available to teachers. It resulted in a frequency result of 5 participants and a cumulative percentage of 55.6 of participants whose scores were similar and who *agreed*.

Interview Questions 8 and 9 examined the time frequency of instructional technology training in a 6-month period. A time of 6 months was chosen based on the schools' instructional technology and professional development plans that usually required professional development within a 3-month interval. The results yielded a frequency of 5 participants responding *undecided* with a cumulative percentage of 33.3 of participants whose scores were similar, suggesting that initial training of instructional technology training was within the last 6 months.

Interview Question 10 examined instructional technology training being available on demand and monitored by the principal. Results yielded a frequency of 2 participants responding *undecided* and a cumulative percentage of 66.7 of participants whose scores were similar and who had the same response of *strongly agree*.

For Interview Questions 11 through 14, participants rated the use or availability of computers in their school buildings. The responses to Interview Question 11 concerned whether the computers were less than 3 years old and had a frequency of 6 participants responding *strongly agree* and a cumulative percentage of 66.7 of participants whose scores were similar and who decided on the same response. Interview Question 12 had a frequency of 9 participants agreeing or strongly agreeing that all computers were CD-ROM capable with a cumulative percentage of 100. Finally, Interview Questions 13 and 14 examined whether building computers were connected to the Internet and a printer. The responses yielded the same frequencies of 6 participants agreeing or strongly agreeing with a cumulative percentage of 100 of participants whose scores were similar.

Summary

With respect to the first two research questions, which investigated the innovativeness characteristics of leadership in schools that have demonstrated passing performance on SOL tests, in general, statistical significance was found at the five levels of characteristics associated with leadership according to individual and organizational innovativeness. Both districts were characterized by statistically significant factors related to innovators, early adopters, early majority, and late majority. Findings showed (a) that, from the organizational innovativeness measures, the innovative characteristic, early adopters, was the most predominant one in both districts and (b) that, from the individual innovativeness measures, early majority was the most predominant one in both districts. Moreover, the results of both districts indicated a statistical significance for passing the SOL assessment tests and gaining accreditation. Frequency analysis from the interviews indicated similarities among participants (leaders).

Interview respondents predominantly agreed or strongly agreed with the statements that involved computers in the school building. These statements dealt with the age of the computers and whether they had CD-ROM capabilities and access to the Internet and printers. Moreover, respondents agreed, to some extent, that the computer software reflected the curricula as required by the SOL. Findings showed that participants agreed that instructional technology was used for lesson preparation, for out-of-class assignments, and that the curriculums were integrated.

Chapter 5: Discussion

This study was designed to examine the phenomena associated with the characteristics of the innovativeness of the leaders and teachers in the two school districts and the overall performance of the students in these school districts on the standardized assessment test. A secondary purpose was to investigate the phenomena associated with certain characteristics of leaders and the perceptions of leaders toward school district innovativeness and school district performance. Finally, this study investigated the use of instructional technology strategies employed by district leaders for growth, development, and training.

Overview

Interview. This researcher used three approaches to gathering data. From the outset, the researcher involved stratification sampling by interviewing 9 principals. The three levels of participating schools were elementary, middle, and high schools. Of the three levels, three interviews were conducted for each level. All 9 principals were interviewed, resulting in 100% participation.

PORGI and II Scale measures. Initially, 200 principals were asked to participate in the study. A total of 184 principals responded to the PORGI for both districts. A total of 193 principals responded to II Scale for both districts. The combined participation rate of 94% was a justifiable rate for interpreting the data results. The reason for the nonrespondents from the second attempt was likely related to absences or conference meetings of principals in different areas of the district. Two surveys were used: the II Scale to measure the innovativeness of participants and the PORGI to measure the innovativeness of the organization as perceived by the individual.

Participation. Participant commitment was very good, and the data results represented their sincerity and dedication. Although only 9 principals were interviewed, the small sample size was considered adequate to interpret the interview data results on the use of instructional technology.

Implications of the Findings

Individuals in any school district may adopt an innovation. The question remains, do individuals adopt at the same time? According to Rogers (2003), the answer is no. Based on this response, Rogers classified innovators into categories and characteristics according to innovativeness. The findings in this study indicated that all categories of adoption--innovator, early adopter, early majority, late majority, and laggard or traditionalists--were categorized by innovativeness characteristics. The findings showed that the measured categories of adoption followed a normal curve or distribution. The bell-shaped curve is an indication that the behavior of leadership in schools is relatively innovative based on continuous variables and that the partitioning of school leaders falls into discrete categories of adoption.

Quantitative Findings

The research questions were evaluated according to the categories of innovativeness of the individual and innovativeness of the organization based on the adoption and use of instructional technology by leaders for training, strategic planning, and implementation. In general, the data collected yielded small differences.

Research Question 1. This research question asked, What are the innovativeness characteristics of leadership in schools that have demonstrated a passing performance on SOL tests? For this question, the researcher examined the innovativeness characteristics of leadership in schools that have a passing performance on the SOL test. For both the inner-city district and the suburban district, the findings showed that individual innovativeness measures identified leadership as mostly displaying the characteristics of the early majority.

Interestingly, participants' results yielded 3% in the category laggards or traditionalists. Laggards or traditionalists are the last ones in a social system to adopt an innovation. They possess almost no opinion leadership and are the most localized of all adopter categories in their outlook. Laggards often base their decisions on what has been done previously. They interact primarily with others who also have relatively traditional values and tend to be suspicious of innovations and of change agents.

Laggards have a relatively lengthy decision process for innovation and are far behind in the awareness of a new idea. Laggards have limited resources and must be certain that a new idea will not fail before they adopt it. Often, a precarious economic position forces the laggard to be extremely cautious about adopting innovations. Laggards, based upon the participants' responses, have very little impact on school leadership.

What may be inferred is that, first, the data results clearly indicated the leadership in schools passing the SOL assessment test was not characterized by the laggard approach to instructional technology but was characterized by innovativeness. Second, both districts had a passing percentage of over 85%, an indication that has a direct relationship to and that is characterized according to the innovativeness of the characteristics of the leadership.

Leadership that promotes instructional technology in the classrooms is a key ingredient to improving student learning (Ruebling et al., 2004). Based on the results examined, the researcher found that the use of instructional technology innovations in both school districts' classrooms demonstrated that school leaders were aware of the potential that instructional technology innovations have for enhancing students' performance (Buck & Horton, 1996).

Research Question 2. This research question asked, What are the innovativeness characteristics of the organization passing state accreditation performance? A complementary question asked, Does the organizational innovativeness of a school have any relationship to the strategies used by leaders to use instructional technology among the members when attaining a passing performance on SOL assessment tests? For both the inner-city and the suburban districts, organizational innovativeness measures identified leadership mostly as early adopters of new technology.

Findings for passing performance showed that the inner-city district had a 90% pass rate and the suburban district had a 93.7% pass rate. These results are a clear representation of the diffusion of innovation theory (Rogers, 2003) and of the positive impact that instructional technology has on a school's performance (Ross et al., 2001).

The responses from participants indicated that the organization's characteristics of innovativeness fell into one or more of the five adoption categories: innovators, early adopters, early majority, late majority, and laggards. However, early adopters predominated. Here again, the result in the laggards or traditionalists category was useful: The 0% response clearly was an indication, supported by other data, that none of the participants believed that the organization's approach toward achieving a passing performance on the SOL test was due to traditional methods.

Interview Findings

The interview analysis was related to Research Questions 3, 4, and 5. The data were combined and analyzed together for the sole purpose of measuring patterns and frequencies of behavior in the same categories for schools whose leaders used instruction technology for strategic growth, development, and training. A list of the results was compiled to reflect the participants' responses according to the use of instructional technology, training, and technological facilities in the schools. Only 9 principals responded to this survey; however, the results indicated that most of the respondents (75%) agreed that instructional technology has been successfully adopted.

Research Question 3. This research question asked, How often is professional staff involved in instructional technology training? The 61.6% of participants who responded positively either strongly agreed or agreed about the adoption and use of instructional technology by classroom teachers, as individual users and as an organization. These percentages were indicative of the behavior patterns experienced by schools with innovative leadership and their implementation of the adoption process associated with the diffusion theory. However, 38.4% of the participant responses concerning the adoption and use of instructional technology as individual users and as an organization were negative.

Research Question 4. This research question asked, What strategies are implemented by organizational leaders for growth, development, and training? The findings showed that 51.9% of the participants agreed or strongly agreed with statements regarding initial training and availability of training. However, 37% of them were undecided as to whether the initial training was over 6 months ago or within the last 6 months and whether training was available on demand. The findings left room for organizational leaders to develop further training strategies for use of instructional technology.

Research Question 5. This research question asked, How are strategies for instructional technology adoption and integration implemented? Findings for this question showed that all 9 respondents agreed that the technological facilities were up to date in that the computers had CD-ROM drives and access to the Internet and printers.

Summary of Findings

Looking back at the results from the quantitative data on the innovativeness of an individual and the organization, the researcher found that responses in the category of laggards or traditionalists might belong to individuals who were not a part of the communication network of the organization. According to Rogers (2003), "Diffusion is a process in which an innovation is communicated through channels over time among members of a social system" (p. 409). Participants' responses indicated a need to develop and support communication networks and social networks that interconnect individuals linked by patterns of flowing information. According to Rogers, from a flow of information, a researcher may develop a pattern of behaviors that have contributed to the passing performance of schools characterized organizationally by innovative leadership. For this study, such leadership was defined as the schools' ability to become accredited by passing the SOL test.

Finally, the data supported the idea that organizational innovativeness contributed to the innovativeness of individuals such as leaders. Leadership categorized by innovativeness contributed to the overall structure of the organization by means of social networks with predictable human behavior in the organization. The passing of the SOL test and the schools' proven performance and accreditation status were clearly related to the behavioral patterns of individuals and the social networks implemented by the leadership.

Limitations

Several limiting factors contributed to the outcome of the study. Initially, the study did not result in a 100% response rate. However, a second attempt resulted in substantial number of participants responding. The study took place during the schools' window of time for SOL testing. A different approach might be to conduct the study before the SOL assessment window. The instrument for interviewing consisted of 15 questions, but only 14 were measurable and used in the study.

The PORGI and II Scale were distributed chiefly by two methods: interoffice school mail and local postal services. For the two instruments, 377 responded out of a possible 400 respondents. The interview outcome was very successful but extremely difficult because of the difficulty in making telephone contact with the participants. Results acquired from this study might be used in further research related to the adoption of instructional technology by leaders in school divisions, as significance was found between leadership characteristics and the use of instructional technology.

Recommendations for Future Research

Several conditions for research might be generalized from the results of this study. First, the study should be lengthened to a year to gather more data from more principals. Additionally, a longitudinal study involving more schools and school districts would increase the validity of the results and reflect the concepts of the diffusion theory (Rogers, 2003). Future research should take into consideration that instructional technology is a topic that will continue to be of interest for years to come.

This critical question should be considered: Does the adoption of instructional technology strategies in the classroom combined with certain leadership characteristics relate to a school's academic performance according to students, not to leaders? This research study was conducted during a time period when technology was controlling the social structures and ways of operating in all social endeavors and in all educational institutions.

Summary

The researcher found that the findings of this study corroborated those of the studies of Rogers (2003). Rogers found that good leadership characteristics in school districts are an advantage when planning for staff development. Moreover, training that effectively trains teachers how to integrate technology into the curricula encourages academic performance. Rogers believed that by training teachers, leaders become opinion leaders through communication channels linked by interconnecting individuals. They establish patterns that provide performance results acceptable to the performance and norms of a school district struggling to meet state accreditation standards. This was certainly the case in the two school districts studied in this applied research project.

References

Abrams, D. P., & Lock, J. (2001). *Computers for twenty-first century educators* (5th ed.). New York: Longman.

Adams, R. (2003). *Perceptions of innovations: Exploring and developing innovation classification*. Unpublished doctoral dissertation, Cranfield University, Cranfield, Bedfordshire, United Kingdom.

Barnett, H. (2001). *Successful K-12 technology planning: Ten essential elements*. East Lansing, MI: National Center for Research on Teacher Learning. (ERIC Document Reproduction Service No. ED457858)

Buck, J. H., & Horton, B. P. (1996). Who's using what and how often: An assessment of the use of computer technology in the classroom. *Florida Journal of Educational Research, 36*(1), 47-61.

Casey, B. H., & Rakes, G. (2002a). An analysis of the influence of technology training on teachers' stages of concern regarding the use of computer technology in schools. *International Journal of Computing in Teacher Education, 18*(4), 124-132.

Casey, B. H., & Rakes, G. (2002b). An analysis of the teachers' concerns toward instructional technology. *International Journal of Educational Technology, 3*(1), 4-13.

Clarke, R. (1991). *A primer in diffusion of innovations theory*. Canberra: Australia National University. Retrieved October 3, 2006, from http://www.anu.edu.au/people/Roger.Clarke/SOS/InnDiff.html

Consortium for School Networking. (2004). What it takes: Essential skills of the K-12 CTO. *Learning and Leading with Technology, 32*(4), 40-45.

Copeland, L. L., & Gray, R. C. (2002). Developing Maryland's technology education leaders for the 21st century: Technology Education Leadership Project (TELP). *Journal of Industrial Teacher Education, 39*(3), 104-121.

Couros, A. (2003). *Innovation, change theory and the acceptance of new technologies: A literature review*. Regina, Saskatchewan, Canada: University of Regina. Retrieved April 12, 2005, from http://educationaltechnology.ca/couros/publications/unpublishedpapers/change_theory.pdf

Dahir, A. C., & Stone, B. C. (2003). Accountability: A M.E.A.S.U.R.E. of the impact school counselors have on student achievement. *Professional School Counseling 6*(3), 214-221.

De Leon, A. G. (2006). The school leadership crisis: Have principals been left behind? *Carnegie Reporter, 4*(1), 1-3.

Dikkers, A. G., Hughes, J. E., & Mcleod, S. (2005). *A bridge to success. The Higher Education Journal, 32*(11), 1-6.

Dillion, S. (2006, July 25). Most states fail demands set out in education law. *New York Times,* p. A14.

Dooley, K. E. (1999). Towards a holistic model for the diffusion of educational technologies: An integrative review of educational innovation studies. *Educational Technology and Society, 2*(4), 35-45. Retrieved October 3, 2007, from http://ifets.ieee.org/periodical/vol_4_99/kim_dooley.html

Feldner, L., & Kincaid, T. (2002). Leadership for technology integration: The role of principals and mentors. *Educational Technology and Society, 5*(1), 75-80. Retrieved July 25, 2006, from http://www.ifets.info/journals/5_1/kincaid.html

Finegan, J. E., Shamian, J., Spencer-Laschinger, H. K., & Wilk, P. (2004). A longitudinal analysis of the impact of workplace empowerment on work satisfaction. *Journal of Organizational Behavior, 25*, 527-544.

Flannery, M. E. (2006, September). Political activism: Packing a punch. *NEA Today, 25,* 30-31.

Fullan, M. (2005). Turnaround leadership. *Educational Forum, 69,* 174-181.

Fullan, M., Bertani, A., & Quinn, J. (2004). New lessons for districtwide reform. *Educational Leadership, 61*(7), 42-46.

Grimes, D. M. (2005). Factors that influenced faculty in the decision to adopt the Internet for instruction at a southeastern United States university. *Dissertation Abstracts International, 66*(04), 1292. (UMI No. 3173571)

Higgins, S., Miller, J., Smith, H. J., & Wall, K. (2005). Interactive whiteboards: Boom or bandwagon? *Journal of Computer Assisted Learning, 21*(2), 91-101.

Hurt, H. T., Joseph, K., & Cook, C. D. (1977). Scales for the measurement of innovativeness. *Human Communication Research, 4*(1), 58-65.

Hurt, H. T., & Teigen, C. W. (1977). The development of a measure of perceived organizational innovativeness. In B. R. Ruben (Ed.), *Communication: Yearbook 1* (pp. 377-385). New Brunswick, NJ: Transaction Books.

Lambert, W. (2004). *Servant leadership qualities of principals, organizational climate, and student achievement: A correlational study.* Unpublished doctoral dissertation, Nova Southeastern University, Fort Lauderdale, FL.

LaRose, R., & Hoag, A. (1996). Organizational adoptions of the Internet and clustering of innovations. *Telematics and Informatics, 13*(1), 49-61.

Leithwood, K. A., & Reihl, C. (2003, April). *What do we already know about successful school leadership?* Paper presented at the annual meeting of the American Educational Research Association, Chicago, IL.

Manterna, L., & Maushak, N. J. (1997). *Iowa Distance Education Alliance: Evaluation report.* Ames: Iowa State University of Science and Education, College of Education. (ERIC Document Reproduction Service No. ED416813)

Marinho, R. M. (2003). How faculty learn to use instructional technology: An exploration of personal experiences. *Dissertation Abstracts International, 65*(02), 431. (UMI No. 3122708)

Marzano, R. J., McNulty, B., & Waters, T. (2004). Leadership that sparks learning. *Educational Leadership, 61*(7), 48-52.

Mazzeo, C. (2003). *The impact of arts education on workforce preparation.* Washington, DC: National Governors Association Center for Best Practices, Economic and Technology Policy Studies. Retrieved on October 3, 2007, from http://www.nga.org/cda/files/050102ARTSED.pdf

Meghabghab, D. B., & Price, C. (1997). *The impact of a technology-rich environment.* East Lansing, MI: National Center for Research on Teacher Learning. (ERIC Document Reproduction Service No. ED412953)

Miech, J. E. (2000). *The necessary gentleman: Francis Keppel's leadership in getting education's act together.* Unpublished master's thesis, Harvard University, Cambridge, MA.

National Center for Education Statistics. (2000). *Teachers' use of computers in school: Stats in brief.* Washington, DC: U.S. Department of Education. Retrieved October 27, 2006, from http://nces.ed.gov/pubs2000/2000090.pdf

Phillips, S. (2006, May 12). Struggling schools face the database crunch (Education supplement). *The Times* (London), p. 20.

Popham, W. J. (2000). *Modern educational measurement: Practical guidelines for educational leaders* (3rd ed.). Needham, MA: Pearson.

Rogers, E. M. (2003). *Diffusion of innovations* (5th ed.). New York: Free Press.

Ross, J. D., McGraw, T. M., & Burdette, K. J. (2001). *Toward an effective use of technology in education: A summary of research.* Charleston, WV: Advancement of Emerging Technologies in Education, Appalachia Educational Laboratory. (ERIC Document Reproduction Service No. ED462963)

Ruebling, C. E., Stow, S. B., Kayona, F. B., & Clarke, N. A. (2004). Instructional leadership: An essential ingredient for improving student learning. *Educational*

Forum, 68, 243-253.

Sanders, M. (2006). Technology education leadership: Observations and reflections. *Technology Teacher, 66*(3), 31-35.

Seels, B., & Richey, R. (1994). *Instructional technology: The definition and domains of the field.* Washington, D.C.: Association for Educational Communications and Technology.

Simonson, M., & Wheeler, S. (2003). *Final report of the evaluation team of the South Dakota Alliance for Distance Education: South Dakota's STAR schools project.* Pierre, SD: South Dakota Department of Education. Retrieved June 23, 2006, from http://www2.plymouth.ac.uk/distancelearning/finalreport.pdf

Shuldman, M. (2004). Superintendent conceptions of institutional conditions that impact teacher technology. *Journal of Research on Technology in Education, 36*, 319-343.

Soars, A., & Soars, T. (2002). The power trail in educational reform. *Educational Forum, 66*, 309-313.

Sunderman, G. L., Orfield, G., & Kim, J. S. (2006, April). Flawed assumptions: How No Child Left Behind fails principals. *Principal Leadership* (High school ed.), *6*, 16-19.

Surry, D. (1997, February). *Diffusion theory and instructional technology.* Paper presented at the annual conference of the Association for Educational Communications and Technology, Albuquerque, NM.

Tetreaut, D. R. (2005). Administrative technology: New rules, new tools. *The Higher Education Journal, 32*(9), 1-5.

Tomei, L. A. (2002). *The technology façade: Overcoming barriers to effective instructional technology.* Boston: Allyn and Bacon.

Virginia Department of Education. (2006a). *Calculation of certain accreditation ratings.* Richmond, VA: Author. Retrieved July 12, 2006, from http://www.pen.k12.va.us/VDOE/Accountability/SOAratings.pdf

Virginia Department of Education. (2006b). *Virginia school report card: Education for life.* Richmond, VA: Author. Retrieved October 26, 2006 from http://www.pen.k12.va.us/VDOE/src/index.shtml

Virginia Education Association. (2005). *Survey: Teachers, principals see situations differently.* Richmond, VA: Author. Retrieved April 29, 2006, from http://www.veaweteach.org/articles_print.asp?ContentID=1143

Vitale, D. J. (2005). Developing technology integrators: The role of professional development for instructional technology integration. *Dissertation Abstracts*

International, 65(05), 1539. (UMI No. 3175437)

Voogt, J., Moonrn, B., Akker, J. V. D., & Almekinders, M. (2005). A "blended" in-service arrangement for classroom technology integration: Impacts on teachers and students. *Computer in Human Behavior, 21*, 523-539.

Wepner, B. S. (2006). Testing gone amok: Leave no teachers behind. *Teacher Education Quarterly, 33*(1), 135-149.

Wilson, T. A. (2001). *School Accountability for Learning and Teaching (SALT): The accountability program of the Rhode Island Department of Education.* Providence, RI: Rhode Island Department of Education.

Appendix A

Calculation of Accreditation Ratings in
Standards of Accreditation

Calculation of Accreditation Ratings in
Standards of Accreditation

Subject	Grade 3 (%)	Grade 4 (%)*	Grade 5 (%)	Grades 6–12 (%)
English	75	70	75	70
Mathematics	70	70	70	70
Science	50	--	70	70
History/social science	50	--	70	70

Note. Benchmarks are tests administered in 2005–2006 through 2008–2009 for ratings earned in 2006–2007 through ratings earned in 2009–2010 (standards of accreditation).
*2006–2007 ratings only.

Appendix B

Accrediting Public Schools (Verified Credits)

Accrediting Public Schools (Verified Credits)

Discipline area	Standard units of credit required	Verified credits required
English	4	2
Mathematics	3	1
Laboratory science	3	1
History and social sciences	3	1
Health and physical education	2	
Fine arts or practical arts career and technical education	1	
Electives	6	
Student selected test		1
Total	22	6

Appendix C

Bell-Shaped Curve

Bell-Shaped Curve

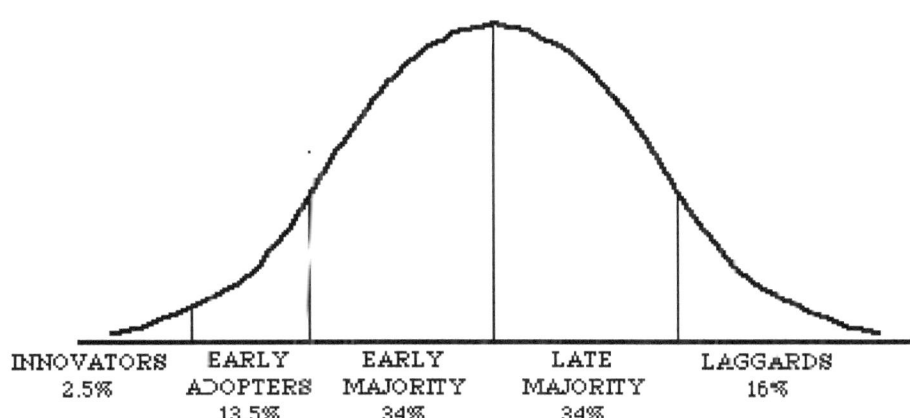

Bell-shaped curve showing categories of individual innovativeness and percentages within each category.

Note. From "Diffusion Theory and Instructional Technology," by D. Surry, 1997, paper presented at the annual conference of the Association for Educational Communications and Technology, Albuquerque, NM. Copyright 1997 by D. Surry. Reprinted with permission.

Appendix D

Perceived Organizational Innovativeness Scale

Perceived Organizational Innovativeness Scale

An innovation is an idea, practice, or object that is perceived as new by an individual or other unit of adoption (like an organization). People and organizations vary a great deal in their "innovativeness." Innovativeness has to do with how early in the process of adoption of new ideas, practices, etc. that the individual or organization is likely to accept a change.

The organizational innovativeness scale was designed to measure a member of an organization's perception of the organization's orientation toward change. Research has indicated that this orientation is associated with several patterns of behavior (including communication) relating to change. The organizational innovativeness scale has been found to be highly reliable (alpha above .90) and the predictive validity is very good.

Directions: Organizations respond to change in different ways. The statements below refer to some of the ways members of organizations perceive their organizations to be. Please indicate the degree to which you agree that the statement describes your organization. In the blank just before the statement, indicate whether you (1) *strongly disagree* (2); *disagree* (3); *undecided*; (4) *agree* (5); or *strongly agree*.

My organization

_____ 1. is cautious about accepting new ideas.

_____ 2. is a leader among other organizations.

_____ 3. is suspicious of new ways of thinking.

_____ 4. is very inventive.

_____ 5. is often consulted by other organizations for advice and information.

_____ 6. is skeptical of new ideas.

_____ 7. is creative in its method of operation.

_____ 8. is usually one of the last of its kind to change to a new method of operation.

_____ 9. is considered one of the leaders of its type.

_____ 10. is receptive to new ideas.

_____ 11. is challenged by new ideas.

_____ 12. follows the belief that "the old way of doing things is the best."

_____ 13. is very original in its operational procedures.

_____ 14. responds slowly to necessary changes.

_____ 15. is reluctant to adopt new ways of doing things until other organizations have used them successfully.

_____ 16. is a frequent initiator of new methods of operations.

_____ 17. is slow to change.

_____ 18. rarely involves employees in the decision-making process.

_____ 19. maintains good communication between supervisors and employees.

_____ 20. is influential with other organizations.

_____ 21. seeks out new ways of doing things.

_____ 22. rarely trusts new ideas and ways of functioning.

_____ 23. never satisfactorily explains to employees the reasons for procedural changes.

_____ 24. frequently tries out new ideas.

_____ 25. is willing and ready to accept outside help when necessary.

Scoring Procedure

Step 1. Add the scores for the following items: 1, 3, 6, 8, 12, 14, 15, 17, 18, 22, and 23.

Step 2. Add the scores for the following items: 2, 4, 5, 7, 9, 10, 11, 13, 16, 19, 20, 21, 24, and 25.

Step 3. Complete the following formula. PORGI = 66 + total from Step 2 - total from Step 1.

Scores can range between 25 and 125.

Scores above 110 indicate that the organization can be classified as innovative.

Scores between 91 and 110 indicate the organization is an early adopter.

Scores between 71 and 90 indicate the organization is in the early majority.

Scores between 50 and 70 indicate the organization is in the late majority.

Scores below 50 indicate the organization can be classified as a laggard or traditional.

Generally, organizations that score above 90 are high in innovativeness. Those scoring below 50 are low in innovativeness. Those scoring between 50 and 90 are moderate in innovativeness.

Note. From "The Development of a Measure of Perceived Organizational Innovativeness" by H. T. Hurt and C. W. Teigen. In *Communication: Yearbook 1* (pp. 377-385) by B. R. Ruben (Ed.), 1977, New Brunswick, NJ: Transaction Books. Copyright 1977 by H. T. Hurt and C. W. Teigen. Adapted with permission.

Appendix E

Individual Innovativeness Scale

Individual Innovativeness Scale

An innovation is an idea, practice, or object that is perceived as new by an individual or other unit of adoption (like an organization). People and organizations vary a great deal in their "innovativeness." Innovativeness has to do with how early in the process of adoption of new ideas, practices, etc. that the individual or organization is likely to accept a change.

The II Scale was designed to measure individuals' orientations toward change. Research has indicated that this orientation is associated with several communication variables. The II instrument has been found to be highly reliable and the predictive validity is good.

Directions: People respond to their environment in different ways. The statements below refer to some of the ways people can respond. Please indicate the degree to which each statement applies to you by marking whether you *strongly disagree* (1); *disagree* (2); *neutral* (3); *agree* (4); *strongly disagree* (5). Please work quickly. There are no right or wrong answers. Just record your first impression.

_____ 1. My peers often ask me for advice or information.

_____ 2. I enjoy trying new ideas.

_____ 3. I seek out new ways to do things.

_____ 4. I am generally cautious about accepting new ideas.

_____ 5. I frequently improvise methods for solving a problem when an answer is not apparent.

_____ 6. I am suspicious of new inventions and new ways of thinking.

_____ 7. I rarely trust new ideas until I can see whether the vast majority of people around me accept them.

_____ 8. I feel that I am an influential member of my peer group.

_____ 9. I consider myself to be creative and original in my thinking and behavior.

_____ 10. I am aware that I am usually one of the last people in my group to accept something new.

_____ 11. I am an inventive kind of person.

_____ 12. I enjoy taking part in the leadership responsibilities of the group I belong to.

_____ 13. I am reluctant about adopting new ways of doing things until I see them working for people around me.

_____ 14. I find it stimulating to be original in my thinking and behavior.

_____ 15. I tend to feel that the old way of living and doing things is the best way.

_____ 16. I am challenged by ambiguities and unsolved problems.

_____ 17. I must see other people using innovations before I will consider them.

_____ 18. I am receptive to new ideas.

_____ 19. I am challenged by unanswered questions.

_____ 20. I often find myself skeptical of new ideas.

Scoring Procedure

Step 1: Add the scores for items 4, 6, 7, 10, 13, 15, 17, and 20.

Step 2: Add the scores for items 1, 2, 3, 5, 8, 9, 11, 12, 14, 16, 18, and 19.

Step 3: Complete the following formula: II = 42 + total score for Step 2 - total score for Step 1.

Scores above 80 are classified as innovators.

Scores between 69 and 80 are classified as early adopters.

Scores between 57 and 68 are classified as early majority.

Scores between 46 and 56 are classified as late majority.

Scores below 46 are classified as laggards/traditionalists.

In general, people who score above 68 are considered highly innovative, and people who score below 64 are considered low in innovativeness.

Note. From "Scales for the Measurement of Innovativeness," by H. T. Hurt, K. Joseph, and C. D. Cock, 1977, *Human Communication Research, 4*, pp. 58-65. Copyright 1977 by H. T Hurt, K. Joselph, and C. D. Cook. Adapted with permission.

Appendix F

Interview Technology Checklist

Interview Technology Checklist

You will be asked 13 questions, all questions relate to instructional technology only in your school building. Each question is based on a scale of 1 to 4: 1 = *strongly disagree*, 2 = *undecided*, 3 = *agree*, and a 4 = *strongly agree*.

1. Instructional technology is always used by all teachers in your building.

    (Response 1: _____)

2. Would you say that classroom teachers use instructional technology for

    a. grading? (Response 2: _____)

    b. lesson preparation? (Response 3: _____)

    c. out-of-class assignment? (Response 4: _____)

    d. professional development? (Response 5: _____)

3. Curriculums are integrated with instructional technology lesson plans.

    (Response 6: _____)

4. Does the software found on your computers reflect current SOL curricula?

    a. Computer software is available and based on teachers' input.

    (Response 7: _____)

    b. Computer software that has been purchased is available for teachers.

    (Response 8: _____)

5. What is the extent of instructional technology training received by teachers?

    a. Initial training of instructional technology is over 6 months old.

    (Response 9: _____)

    b. Initial training of instructional technology is within the last 6 months.

    (Response 10: _____)

    c. Training classes are available on demand and monitored by the principal.

(Response 11: _____)

6. Rate the computers in school building.

   a. Less than 3 years old. (Response 12: _____)

   b. CD-ROM capable (Response 13: _____)

   c. Most are connected to the Internet. (Response 14: _____)

   d. Most are connected to a printer. (Response 15: _____)

Appendix G

Interview Log of Contact Information

Interview Log of Contact Information

Leadership position: _____

School code (1-4): _____

School code (4-5): _____

Date: _____

Time: _____

Total interview time: _____

Comments: _____

_____

_____

_____

_____

_____

_____

_____

_____

_____

Interpretation of codes:

1 = high school

2 = middle school

3 = elementary school

4 = pass

5 = fail

www.ingramcontent.com/pod-product-compliance
Lightning Source LLC
Chambersburg PA
CBHW081940170426
43202CB00018B/2962